BEI GRIN MACHT SICH I
WISSEN BEZAHLT

- Wir veröffentlichen Ihre Hausarbeit,
  Bachelor- und Masterarbeit

- Ihr eigenes eBook und Buch -
  weltweit in allen wichtigen Shops

- Verdienen Sie an jedem Verkauf

Jetzt bei www.GRIN.com hochladen
und kostenlos publizieren

Tobias Buchberger

Risk Management - It's role in strategic planning

GRIN Verlag

Bibliografische Information der Deutschen Nationalbibliothek:

Die Deutsche Bibliothek verzeichnet diese Publikation in der Deutschen National-
bibliografie; detaillierte bibliografische Daten sind im Internet über http://dnb.d-
nb.de/ abrufbar.

Impressum:

Copyright © 2009 GRIN Verlag GmbH
Druck und Bindung: Books on Demand GmbH, Norderstedt Germany
ISBN: 978-3-640-70242-8

Dieses Buch bei GRIN:

http://www.grin.com/de/e-book/157097/risk-management-it-s-role-in-strategic-
planning

GRIN - Your knowledge has value

Der GRIN Verlag publiziert seit 1998 wissenschaftliche Arbeiten von Studenten, Hochschullehrern und anderen Akademikern als eBook und gedrucktes Buch. Die Verlagswebsite www.grin.com ist die ideale Plattform zur Veröffentlichung von Hausarbeiten, Abschlussarbeiten, wissenschaftlichen Aufsätzen, Dissertationen und Fachbüchern.

Besuchen Sie uns im Internet:

http://www.grin.com/

http://www.facebook.com/grincom

http://www.twitter.com/grin_com

Risk management

Its role in strategic planning

Växjö University
Strategic Thinking

Tobias Buchberger

Management Summary

In organizations are plenty of IS/IT investments to choose from. All of these opportunities compete for the limited resources of the organization. The process of risk management which can be divided into the four phases of Identification, Quantification, Management/Government and Containment helps to analyze possible risks. This is necessary because every forth IS/IT projects fails[1], because of non identified risks. The aim of Risk Management is to increase the probability of success of IS/IT investments[2], so that the investments drive to the desired outcome and benefits for the organization. In the following the four steps of risk management will be illustrated with an example of a logistic company which has to decide on two investments. Additionally the role of risk management in strategic planning will be examined.

---

[1] C.f.: [Pütt2009].
[2] C.f.: [WaPe2002] p.462.

Table of contents

List of abbreviations

Abbreviation	Description
CIO	Chief Information Officer
CRM	Customer Relationship Management
ERP	Enterprise Resource Planning
IS	Information System
IT	Information Technology

Table of figures

1 The concept of risk management

When it comes to the decision of investing in new developments or significant enhancements in existing IT/IS (Information Technology/ Information System) systems, the expected benefits of the investments have to be established, the costs of the systems have to be justified, the involvement of technology and business changes and the priorities to individual developments across the portfolio have to be allocated.[3] Apart from that one of the main issues of the investment decision in IT/IS systems, is the assessment of the risk. Risk, which is in the failure oriented definition the negative deviation from expectancy[4], has to be assessed in order to revise the viability of the investment to deliver all of the benefits which were expected[5]. The reasons for failure of an investment in IT/IS systems can be divided into five domains. Beside the technical, data and user failure there are organizational failures[6] and failure in the business environment which this paper focuses on[7], because they are the factors with the highest risk[8]. Organizational failures occur if ISs satisfy the functional needs but do not satisfy the organizational or business needs[9]. For example, a storage-IS, which contains the amounts of goods in a storage, fails to meet the needs of accounting because it does not contain monetary values for the goods. Failures in the business environment result if systems do not assists internal and external business requirements. This lack of support could be ascribed to changing business practices or changes in the business strategy which cause a gap between target state and actual state of the IS/IT portfolio.[10]

These two facts comprise the most potential risk in IS/IT projects. But in most of the projects organizational failures and failures in the business environment are not considered as risky. This is due to the disability to address and identify risks in these categories which could threaten the achievement of the desired outcome. Especially in strategic investments of IS/IT the consequences of failure are significant and the assessment of risks is becoming more difficult.[11]

1.1 Steps of application

The process of risk management, which is defined as the systematical handling of risk[12], can be divided into four phases: Identification, Quantification, Management/Government and Containment[13].

---

3 c.f.: [WaPe2002] p.420.
4 C.f.: [ScLi2002] p.183.
5 C.f.: [WaPe2002] p.455.
6 C.f.: [LyHi1987].
7 C.f.: [WaPe2002] p.455.
8 C.f.: [EwPr1994].
9 C.f.: [WaPe2002] p.456.
10 C.f.: [WaPe2002] p.456.
11 C.f.: [WaPe2002] p.456f.
12 C.f.: [AhMa2008] p.11.
13 C.f.: [Höls2002] p.13; [Schi2001] p.13; [Fais2009] p.4.

During the phase of Risk Identification the risks are defined and categorized[14]. IS/IT investments have to be reviewed if they satisfy the organizational functions and are appropriate to the business environment and strategy of the organization. This step is the basis of the following steps and has a high importance. The risk quantification conduces to assess the extent of risk. This step can be executed with the help of a checklist which divides the investment into the four parts of

    a. Which changes are involved?[15]
    b. Is the organization ready for the change?[16]
    c. How will the organization react for the change?[17]
    d. How dynamic is the context of the change?[18]

Constitutive on the risk quantification, decisions have to be made how to deal with risk. Liermann mentions four possibilities, avoiding, decreasing, transferring and taking risk by oneself, to deal with risk.[19] Avoiding risk denotes that the decision maker abdicates the IS/IT investment. This could be reasonable if the investment in an IS/IT project is rated with a high risk and the damage caused by a fail is huge. The second choice is to reduce risk with retaliatory action. This could be for example warranties, contracts or insurances for investments in IS/IT. Beyond that it is possible to transfer risk by outsourcing IS/IT systems to an external provider which is responsible for it. At least organizations can take the risk by themselves, if the costs for the other arrangements are too high, if arrangements do not exists or if the risk is acceptable.

The decision which of the arrangements to choose, depends upon the result of the quantification process. If 50% of the category factors are 4 or 5 or the average for any category is 4 or 5 the risk should not be taken by oneself[20]. The decision maker should then pick one of the first three arrangements or he should change the development approach in order to reduce the risk.

Unlike the preceding phases before the risk containment is an ex-post analysis to evaluate the decisions and assumption in the former phases[21]. It has to be evaluated if all of the risks have been assessed correctly, if the chosen arrangements have been appropriate and if the investments have been successful. Beyond that stakeholders and the management have to be informed about the success of the investment[22].

---

[14] C.f.: [FaPW2007] p.514.
[15] C.f.: Figure 3 in abbendum.
[16] C.f.: Figure 4 in abbendum.
[17] C.f.: Figure 5 in abbendum.
[18] C.f.: Figure 6 in abbendum.
[19] C.f.: [Lier2009].
[20] C.f.: [WaPe2002] p.461.
[21] C.f.: [Höls2002] p.16.
[22] C.f.: [ScLi2002] p.192.

1.2 Its role in strategic planning

As a part of the "managing investments in Information Systems and Technology process", the aim of risk management is to increase the probability of success of IS/IT investments.[23] Organizations dispose over a portfolio of different IS/IT investments which are considered as new and useful developments. Before money is invested into these opportunities the expected benefits of the investments have to be established, the costs have to be justified, the technology and business changes involved have to be defined and at last the risk of the investment has to be assessed.[24] The last step is necessary to identify the threats and implication which threaten the achievement of the desired benefits of the investment. This enables to initiate appropriate arrangements to reduce the risk to successfully implement the new IS/IT project into the application portfolio.

For most of the IS/IT investments exists opportunity costs. This implies that the money used for an investment could have been used for another and that different investments compete for funds and other resources like time and labour.[25] Additionally the fact that every forth IS/IT project fails[26], increases the demand for an effective risk management to evaluate the critical risks ex-ante and to invest the resources of an organization in those projects which are most promising to deliver the desired outcome and whose risks are manageable. Considering this, risk management can be seen as a process which helps decision makers to pick those investments which will be successful and deliver the desired outcome.

2 Practical Situation

In this chapter a practical situation will be described in which risk management is useful: The CIO (chief information officer) of a half-inferior logistic organization has to decide which of the following two investments he wants to choose. Inside, the organization possesses the needed capabilities and experience to execute the projects. But the willingness of the stakeholders is lower for investment 1 then for investment 2, because the actual solution is still appropriate to fulfill the internal needs. At first the costs, benefits, business and technological changes have to be identified. After this step the risks can be identified, quantified and managed/governed (see chapter 1.2). The Risk Containment is excluded.

[23] C.f.: [WaPe2002] p.462.
[24] C.f.: [WaPe2002] p.420.
[25] C.f.: [WaPe2002] p.462.
[26] C.f.: [Pütt2009].

4

	Investment 1	Investment 2
Description	Replacement of the antiquated ERP (Enterprise Resource Planning) Software with SAP R/3	Implementation of CRM (Customer Relationship Management) software
costs	10 million	8 million
benefits	• Exchange of data with suppliers and customers • Data exchange with other internal IS • Extensive customization of the software to the organizational needs	• Advancement of the maintenance of customer relationships • Analysis of buying patterns • Identification of customer potentials and disaffection • Advancement of customer orientation • Customer recruitment
Business changes	• Changes in business processes and workflows • Retraining of employees/users	• inurnment of employees to work with new software • Usage of CRM software to make decisions about how to deal with customers
Technological changes	• Migration of data from the old to the new system • reassessment of data • Interfaces to other IS • New client software	• Central data store for customer data • New client software

Figure 1 - Investments comparison

2.1 Phase 1 – Risk Identification

Investment 1	Investment 2
Organizational: • Acceptance of users • skepticalness of stakeholders • Huge impact on operational business	*Organizational:* • Wrong decisions because of wrong analysis • Acceptance of users

• Critical system	Technical:
Technical:	• Irregular data management of users
• Migration of data	• Data loses in central data store
• Data losing	• Compatibility to other IS
• Interfaces to other systems	
• Security issues	
• Ability to run on clients	

Figure 2 - Risk Identification of investments

2.2 Phase 2 - Risk Quantification

The average score of Category A: Kind of change is satisfying for both investments. But Investment A has in more than 50% of the factors a rating higher than 3.[27] This is an indicator that the success of Investment 1 is threatened[28]. With a score of 2,22 and 2,11 for both investments the organization is ready for the change which the investments include.[29] The reaction of the stakeholders is positive for investment 2 and negative for the first.[30] This means that there will be problems to establish the new ERP system in the organization. At last it is to see that both investments are ready for a contextual change.[31]

The risk quantification shows that investment 1 is more risky than the second. This means that investment 1 is more likely to fail. In the next Phase solutions will be presented which help to reduce the risk of the first investment. Investment 2 could be chosen, because the risk is adequate and there is no urgent need for arrangements to reduce the risk.

2.3 Phase 3 – Risk Management/Government

Avoiding risk

The avoidance of the first investment is to advice, because the risk of failure is high. There are many stakeholders who do not support the investment and the impact of the change for the user and the business is huge.

Decrease risk

The risks for the first investment could be decreased by progressively implement the new ERP IS in the organization. In this way stakeholders could get convinced that the new ERP system is more useful

---

[27] C.f.: Figure 7 in abbendum.
[28] C.f.: [WaPe2002] p.461.
[29] C.f.: Figure 7 in abbendum.
[30] C.f.: Figure 7 in abbendum.
[31] C.f.: Figure 7 in abbendum.

than the old one and the impact on the business would be smaller if the system would be implemented in only a few departments, to test it. Additionally the connection with systems of suppliers and customers could be canceled. This would reduce the impact on the business as well as the degree of the change and the technological innovation.

Transferring risk

The assignment of another company to implement the ERP system is not advisable because the experience and capabilities available. Additionally the assignment of an external company would not lower the risk.

Taking risk by oneself

The organization could decide to take the risk on themselves. This would imply that they have to deal with all of the consequences of a failure on their own and are not able to reduce the risk. The organization should abandon to take the risk by themselves, because it is too high.

2.4 Conclusion

From the point of view of the risk management the logistic organization should choose the second investment. The first investment has a higher risk and is more likely to fail. It is possible to lower the risk of the first investment by reducing the targeted benefits and by implementing the new ERP system incrementally to convince the stakeholder from the importance of the investment.

Apart from the risk management point of view there can be other aspects which weight more and could influence the decision to invest in the first investment rather than in the second. This could be for example the need to connect the system to a very important customer or supplier, an aging ERP system, new features and functions of the new system, preferences of the management or legal specifications. Risk Management is only a process to evaluate investments. The decision which investments will be chosen can be based on many other aspects.

List of literature

Abbreviation	Source
[WaPe2002]	**Ward, J./Peppard, J.**: Strategic Planning for Information Systems, 3rd edition, John Wiley & Sons, Chichester, 2002.
[LyHi1987]	**Lyytinen, K./Hirschheim, R.**: Information systems failures: A survey and classification of the empirical literature, in: Oxford Surveys in Information Technology, Vol. 4, 1987, 257–309.
[EwPr1994]	**Ewusi-Mensah/K.,Przasnyski, Z.H.**: Factors contributing to the abandonment of information systems development projects, in: Journal of Information Technology, Vol. 9, 1994.
[ScLi2002]	**Schierenbeck, H./Lister, M.**: Risikomanagement im Rahmen der wertorientierten Unternehmenssteuerung. In: Hölscher, R./Elfgen, R.: Herausforderung Risikomanagement: Identifikation, Bewertung und Steuerung industrieller Risiken, Gabler Verlag, Wiesbaden, S. 181-204, 2002.
[Höls2002]	**Hölscher, R.**: Von der Versicherung zur integrativen Risikobewältigung: Die Konzeption eines modernen Risikomanagements, In: Hölscher, R./Elfgen, R.: Herausforderung Risikomanagement - Identifikation, Bewertung und Steuerung industrieller Risiken, Gabler Verlag, Wiesbaden, S. 3-32, 2002.
[Schi2001]	**Schierenbeck, H.**: Ertragsorientiertes Bankmanagement - Band 2: Risiko-Controlling und integrierte Rendite-/Risikosteuerung, Gabler Verlag, Wiesbaden, 2001.
[Fais2009]	**Faisst, U.**: Ein Modell zur Steuerung operationeller Risiken in IT-unterstützten Bankprozessen, in the Internet: http://www.wiwi.uni-augs-burg.de/bwl/buhl/dyn/root_kernkompetenzzentrum/40Publikationen/pdf/wi-138.pdf?rnd=9491, access: 26.11.2009.
[FaPW2007]	**Faisst, U./Prokein, O./Wegmann, N.**: Ein Modell zur dynamischen

	Investitionsrechnung von IT-Sicherheitsmaßnahmen. In: **Zeitschrift für Betriebswirtschaft**, 77 (5), S. 511-538, 2007.
[Lier2009]	**Liermann, F.:** Risikomanagement. Lehreinheit 6 - Risikopolitische Maßnahmen: Risikovermeidung, -verminderung, -transferierung und – überwachung, in the Internet: http://www.fh-frankfurt.de/de/.media/~liermann/organisationstheorie_le_6_password.pdf, access: 28.11.2009.
[Pütt2009]	**Pütter, C.:** Gescheiterte Projekte: IT-Experten stehen sich selbst im Weg, in the Internet: http://www.cio.de/strategien/projekte/839069/index.html, access: 29.11.2009.
[AhMa2008]	**Ahrendts, F./Marton, A.:** IT-Risikomanagementleben!. Wirkungsvolle Umsetzung für Projekte in der Softwareentwicklung, 1st edition, Springer Verlag, Berlin Heidelberg, 2008.

3 Addendum

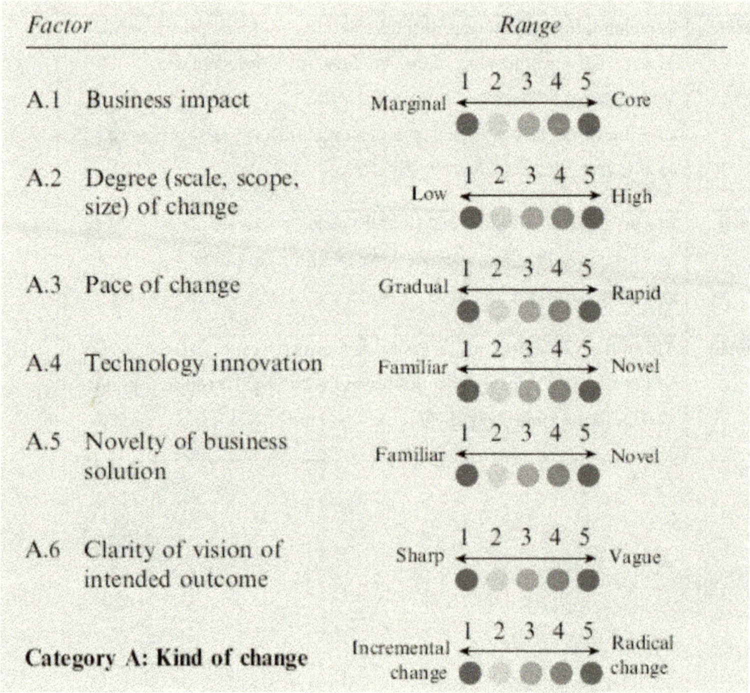

Factor	Range

A.1 Business impact — Marginal 1 2 3 4 5 Core

A.2 Degree (scale, scope, size) of change — Low 1 2 3 4 5 High

A.3 Pace of change — Gradual 1 2 3 4 5 Rapid

A.4 Technology innovation — Familiar 1 2 3 4 5 Novel

A.5 Novelty of business solution — Familiar 1 2 3 4 5 Novel

A.6 Clarity of vision of intended outcome — Sharp 1 2 3 4 5 Vague

Category A: Kind of change — Incremental change 1 2 3 4 5 Radical change

Figure 3 – Kind of change[32]

[32] [WaPe2002] p.459.

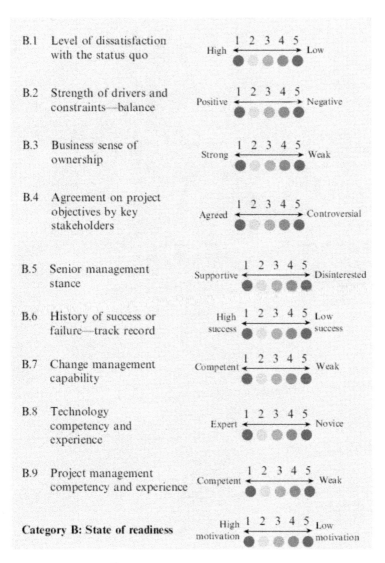

B.1   Level of dissatisfaction with the status quo

B.2   Strength of drivers and constraints—balance

B.3   Business sense of ownership

B.4   Agreement on project objectives by key stakeholders

B.5   Senior management stance

B.6   History of success or failure—track record

B.7   Change management capability

B.8   Technology competency and experience

B.9   Project management competency and experience

Category B: State of readiness

Figure 4 - State of readiness[33]

[33] [WaPe2002] p.459f.

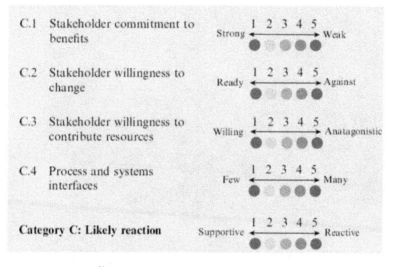

Figure 5 - Likely reaction[34]

---
[34] [WaPe2002] p.460.

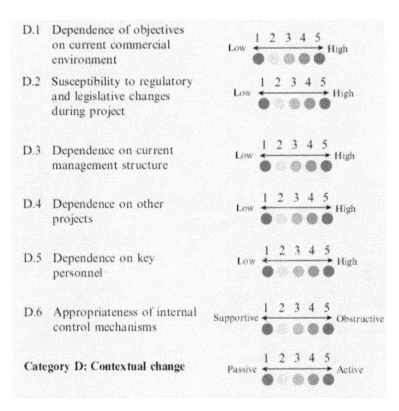

Figure 6 - Contextual change[35]

	Investment 1	Investment 2
Category A: Kind of change	3,83	3,1
A.1 Business impact	5	3
A.2 Degree (scale, scope, size) of change	5	4
A.3 Pace of change	4	3
A.4 Technology innovation	4	4

[35] [WaPe2002] p.460f.

A.5 Novelty of business solution	3	3
A.6 Clarity of vision of intended outcome	2	2
Category B: State of readiness	2,22	2,11
B.1 Level of dissatisfaction with the status quo	5	5
B.2 Strength of drivers and constraints—balance	2	2
B.3 Business sense of ownership	1	3
B.4 Agreement on project objectives by key stakeholders	4	2
B.5 Senior management stance	2	2
B.6 History of success or failure—track record	1	2
B.7 Change management capability	1	1
B.8 Technology competency and experience	1	1
B.9 Project management competency and experience	1	1
Category C: Likely reaction	4	2
C.1 Stakeholder commitment to benefits	4	2
C.2 Stakeholder willingness to change	4	2
C.3 Stakeholder willingness to contribute resources	3	1
C.4 Process and systems interfaces	5	3
Category D: Contextual change	2,5	2,33
D.1 Dependence of objectives on current	3	3

commercial environment		
D.2 Susceptibility to regulatory and legislative changes during project	1	1
D.3 Dependence on current management structure	2	2
D.4 Dependence on other projects	3	2
D.5 Dependence on key personnel	4	4
D.6 Appropriateness of internal control mechanisms	2	2

Figure 7 - Quantification of example